Original title:
The Ocean's Hidden Pulse

Copyright © 2025 Creative Arts Management OÜ
All rights reserved.

Author: Franklin Stone
ISBN HARDBACK: 978-1-80587-429-4
ISBN PAPERBACK: 978-1-80587-899-5

Echoes of a Subaquatic Symphony

Bubbles dance with giggles in the blue,
Fish in tuxedos, what a sight to view!
Crabs with a beat, tap their castanet claws,
While seaweed sways, breaking all the laws.

Starfish play chess on the sandy floor,
Whales sing karaoke, we shout for more!
Jellyfish float, glowing like balloons,
An underwater party that ends too soon!

Pulsations of the Waterfloor

The seaweed waltzes like it knows a tune,
Octopuses juggling, they're quite the boon!
Seahorses spin, in an awkward ballet,
While dolphins pop popcorn, hip-hip-hooray!

Clams clap their shells, marching in a row,
Turtles on scooters, they move nice and slow!
Krill with kazoo, lead an aquatic show,
With jellyfish flashlights, it's never a no-go!

The Secret Symphony of Salinity

Coral conductors wave with vibrant grace,
Fish all around them, join in the race!
A clam plays the tuba, with all of its might,
While sea sponges dance in the glowing moonlight.

Anemones cheer, with confetti of foam,
The floor is a dance hall, the sea is their home!
With a splash and a swish, they twirl to the beat,
Fins slap the rhythm, it's quite the retreat!

Ancient Rhythms of the Sea Bed

Crustaceans trombone, performing their rap,
With barnacles beatboxing, time for a nap!
Seashells are the drums, echoing loud,
Playing harmonies under a wave-loving crowd.

The sea anemone twirls, with colors so bright,
While fish throw confetti, oh what a sight!
Waves whisper secrets of years long gone,
In this merry ocean where we all belong!

Whispers Beneath the Tides

A crab wearing shades struts with pride,
Fish giggle as they try to hide.
Waves tell jokes that make them squeal,
The sea's a stage, a grand reveal.

Seaweed dances in a silly spree,
Jellyfish float like balloons, carefree.
Starfish gather for a comedy show,
While the dolphins chuckle down below.

Currents of the Unseen

A sneaky eel plays peek-a-boo,
Shells gossip about what fish can do.
An octopus juggles krill with flair,
While seahorses spin without a care.

Underwater entities take their plunge,
Catching bubbles as they laugh and lunge.
A clam's pun saves the day once more,
As bubbles rise from a laughing floor.

Rhythm of the Deep Blue

Turtles groove to an underwater beat,
Finding rhythm in their flippered feet.
Clams clap shells to the sound of a tune,
While sea cucumbers strut by the moon.

Anglerfish laugh at their own strange light,
Playing hide and seek in the dead of night.
Whales sing choruses of silly rhymes,
Echoing through the depths without any crimes.

Secrets of the Abyss

Down where squids paint the waves with ink,
They pop out jokes quicker than you think.
A pufferfish blows up with glee,
Telling tales of what he can't really be.

Under the waves, the humor flows,
With every splash, a punchline grows.
Anemones wiggle, tickling some fish,
Creating ripples of laughter that swish.

A Tidal Tale of Unspoken Lore

The fish were all in line, so neat,
A school that danced to a funny beat.
Turtles laughed at the jelly's sway,
They thought they'd start a new ballet.

A crab with shades, oh what a sight,
Said, "Dance with me, I'll feel just right!"
But he tripped on sand and fell with a splash,
The fish all giggled, oh what a crash!

From coral homes, they chimed in cheer,
Sardines wiggled without any fear.
A seahorse tapped, with flair and finesse,
"We must throw a party, no need to impress!"

The mullets brought snacks, some seaweed pies,
While the crabs served drinks, oh what a surprise!
The barnacles joined with their crusty old tunes,
They partied till dawn, 'neath the light of the moons.

Pearl-Laden Mysteries of the Deep

Deep down where the sea cucumbers squish,
A clam made a wish for a tasty dish.
He called to a shrimp for a recipe old,
"Let's cook up something, oh, so bold!"

The shrimp wiggled, with a gleam in his eye,
"Let's toss in some algae and give it a try!"
But the clam said, "Wait! I can't take the heat!"
And quickly retreated, preferring to eat.

An octopus brought his best magic hands,
He juggled the shells on the soft ocean sands.
With eight arms a-swirling, he caused quite a show,
But alas! One slipped and went splat, oh no!

The fishes all cheered for the daring display,
As bubbles of laughter began to array.
In the theatre of tides, they found delight,
In this pearl-laden jest, they danced through the night.

Reflections in Liquid Shadows

The waves chat softly with the sand,
As crabs perform dance, quite unplanned.
Fish giggle as they swim so fast,
While starfish ponder their deep spell cast.

Seagulls play tag, swooping in flight,
While dolphins do somersaults with delight.
Under the sun, all is a blur,
As kelp sways gently, the perfect stir.

Siren Songs of Solitude

In the calm blue, a harp plays sweet,
Mermaids chat about their next treat.
Shells gossip softly, along the shore,
With tales of crabs that we can't ignore.

The tides keep rhythm like a dance floor,
While plankton swirl, forever explore.
Seaweed shakes its leafy attire,
As fish strut by, wearing their quire.

Secrets Swirling in Brine

Under the surface, whispers abound,
As playful octopuses prance all around.
Jellyfish float like fancy balloons,
While turtles keep time to the wavy tunes.

Coral reefs chuckle, in colors so bright,
As curious flounders dive left and right.
The clownfish laugh, a jester's delight,
While shrimp tell tales throughout the night.

Beneath the Surface

Hidden below, the laughter ignites,
Where sea cucumbers wear silly tights.
With bubbles and giggles, the current does swirl,
And walruses slide in a blubbery whirl.

Seahorses dance like they're at a ball,
While fish toss jokes, giving it their all.
The sea floor is a comedy stage,
Where every critter has a script to engage.

Stories Slumber

At dawn, the tide shares its sleepy tales,
Of cheeky dolphins and shipwrecked gales.
Seashells listen with perked up ears,
As they giggle away the ancient fears.

Sandy dunes chuckle at the lost toys,
While crabby pals make their own noise.
Waves lap gently, snoring along,
In this watery world, where we all belong.

Songs of Sediment and Sand

Bubbles dance with fishy glee,
While crabs chase dreams of being free.
Seaweed waves with silly grace,
Sandcastles grin in a sandy race.

Jellyfish juggle with a flip,
Starfish cheer with a little dip.
Mollusks hum a tune so bright,
As dolphins dive and take to flight.

The Heart of the Abyss

Squid in tuxedos waltz and twirl,
Octopus chefs give the sea a whirl.
Fish in bowties throw a bash,
While clams serve up a lightning flash.

Seahorses hold a courtly chat,
Discussing styles like what to wear, a hat?
Eels with jokes that give a shock,
Wave to turtles, knock-knock!

Threads of Stringent Waves

Crabs in a band, they strum and play,
With mixing tunes as they sway.
Oysters giggle and wink with cheer,
Weird fish tell tales you just can't hear.

A seagull croons a silly sound,
While plankton jiggles all around.
The tide rolls in with a playful sigh,
As starfish spin and take to the sky.

Fluid Secrets of the Deep Blue

Fish with colors so rich and wild,
Peek and practice like a child.
Whales sing songs that make fish giggle,
While sea cucumbers just wriggle.

Coral reefs play hide and seek,
Encouraging fish to frolic and peek.
Turtles race doing backflips galore,
In this laughing sea, who could ask for more?

Lurking Depths and Secrets

In the shadows where fish like to hide,
Mysterious secrets begin to collide.
A turtle in sunglasses, what a surprise!
Just taking a selfie, oh, how time flies.

The crabs wear their hats, prepared for a dance,
While octopuses twirl, given half a chance.
Seahorses giggle at the jellyfish sway,
In this underwater ball, they frolic and play.

Undercurrents of Time

Clocks under the waves tick-tock with flair,
A clam lost its job, now sings in despair.
Starfish have parties on the sandy floor,
Counting their arms, they can't count anymore.

Waves like a comedy, splashing around,
With dolphins that juggle, they never fall down.
Time in the deep seems silly and grand,
With bubbles as bursts of laughter on sand.

Veins of the Sea

Coral reefs blush in colors so bright,
With fish telling jokes, it's a vibrant sight.
A whale hums a tune, it's quite a show,
While squids ink the script just to let us know.

The seaweed sways like it's caught in a beat,
As clams tap their shells to the rhythm of heat.
Puffers puff up with a theatrical flair,
In the veins of the sea, fun's always in there.

The Silent Choir of the Deep

Bubbles bubble softly like whispers in night,
While sharks lead a choir; oh, what a fright!
A lobster, baritone, clinks his own shell,
As fish holding pitch, try to sing it well.

Anemones sway to the rhythmic piano,
With flounders as dancers, doing the tango.
A sea slug drops notes like a musical prank,
In the silent choir, laughter's the thanks.

Murmurs from the Seafloor

Bubbles pop, fish gossip loud,
Seaweed sways, the sand's a crowd.
Crabs dance jigs in the moonlit glow,
With shells as hats, they steal the show.

Starfish flip, doing acrobatics,
While turtles gossip, oh so dramatic.
An old clam grumbles, it's such a fuss,
But it's just life, beneath the crust.

Beneath the Surface Symphony

A dolphin hums a silly tune,
As octopuses juggle, what a boon!
With a wink and a wiggle, they show their flair,
Even the seaweed joins in the affair.

A shrimp with a top hat sings real high,
While seahorses trot, oh my oh my!
The bass drum's a turtle, steady and slow,
With a crab chorus adding to the show.

Echoes in the Waters

Whales sing songs that sound like snores,
While squids play tag 'round the coral shores.
A pufferfish puffs, thinks it's a star,
While a jellyfish floats, doing bizarre.

The sea cucumbers gossip with grace,
Complaining of shells taking up space.
And if you listen, laugh a bit,
You'll hear the ocean's wit, a perfect fit.

The Heartbeat of Waves

Waves crash down like a wild drum beat,
Seagulls above, they can't find their seat.
A fish in a tux, it's quite a sight,
While eels play leapfrog, just pure delight!

The crabs host parties, complete with snacks,
While sea turtles share tales of their tracks.
A clam opens wide, says, 'What's the scoop?'
And all join in for a water ballet troupe!

Whispers from the Sunken Realm

Bubbles giggle, swirling round,
Seaweed dances, never bound.
Fish in tux, they flaunt their style,
Crabs pull pranks, with cheeky smile.

Anemones wave, don't you dare touch,
They're like that friend who loves to clutch.
Octopus juggling, oh what a sight,
Prawns throw parties that last all night.

Clownfish telling knock-knock jokes,
While sardines form their little folks.
A treasure chest sings in delight,
Sea snails move slowly, but not out of spite.

Mermaids giggle, flip their tail,
Trying to find a new fairy tale.
With every wave, a chuckle resounds,
In this kingdom where laughter abounds.

Coral Choreography of Life

Corals sway to a rhythm divine,
With starfish tapping, they all align.
Seahorses twirl in a silly embrace,
While plankton tosses confetti in space.

A turtle slides with a grin so wide,
In this dance-floor, there's nowhere to hide.
Clams snap shut, a comedy show,
Do sea cucumbers wiggle? Who knows?

In the coral ballet, a fish leaps high,
But oops! Lands right where the starfish lie.
Laughing gulls above start to cheer,
Even the jellyfish join in to steer.

With every flip, there's a giggly splash,
Sideways swim, oh what a dash!
In the ocean's groove, humor flows,
A hilarious spectacle as laughter grows.

Dreams Adrift on Aquatic Breezes

Waves whisper secrets, jokes from afar,
Surfboards ride like distant stars.
A dolphin grins, flips in delight,
While crabs tap dance under moonlight.

Seashells gather for gossip and tea,
"Did you see the octopus? He spilled his spree!"
Little planes of fish zoom by fast,
While sea urchins ponder, "How long will this last?"

The tide rolls in, wearing a crown,
With starfish making faces, upside down.
Mermaids chuckle in bubbles so round,
As they plot pranks on sardines around.

Snorkelers giggling, "Watch out for that shoal!"
"Zebra fish pranks, they're out of control!"
Every wave, an echo of fun,
In this deep blue world where laughter's spun.

The Heartbeat of Salt and Sea

Starfish tapping in a beat so neat,
While pelicans dance on their paddle-shaped feet.
Sardines swirling in a glitzy parade,
Who knew that fish could be so unafraid?

Little shrimps snap selfies on the go,
"Check out my filter—Oh, what a glow!"
With crabs on scooters zooming past,
Life here is a blast, we're having a blast!

Gulls are shouting, "Hey, what's the fuss?"
"Swimming with dolphins, come join us!"
And the seals are laughing, sliding with glee,
As the seaweed whispers, "Don't bother me!"

From sunlit shores to the depths profound,
Every ripple and giggle can surely be found.
In this salty realm where jokes never cease,
The heartbeat of laughter brings sweet release.

Waves of Unspoken Stories

The waves roll in with a giggle,
Crabs dance like they're at a wiggle.
A fish sneezes, makes a splash,
As seaweed sways in a flashy bash.

Seagulls squawk with a comic flair,
While starfish lounge without a care.
A dolphin's joke goes overboard,
And clam shells chuckle, never bored.

As tides turn tales beneath the sun,
Even barnacles join in the fun.
The rhythm rolls, a whimsical tune,
Underneath the light of the moon.

Giant squids wear silly hats,
While turtles trade their beachside chats.
Laughter bubbles, rolls, and flows,
In a world where the fun just grows.

The Depths' Quiet Allegro

Bubbles waltz in a playful swirl,
An octopus gives a tender twirl.
Jellyfish bob like they're on a spree,
In this ballet deep beneath the sea.

Seashells sing in a shrill refrain,
While shrimp bring shrimp cocktails for the gain.
Anemones bob, compose a song,
With rhythm that feels cheeky and strong.

Grouper calls with a grandiose shout,
While porpoises play a game of doubt.
A conch shell and a clam share a laugh,
In this underwater epitaph.

With every pulse and every beat,
Fish in tuxedos tap their feet.
Corals high-five with a gentle sway,
In the depths, where humor holds sway.

Rippled Reveries

Waves whisper tales of sunken ships,
While mermaids tease with playful quips.
Crabs tell jokes that make you chuckle,
With every ripple, life's a huddle.

Bubbles rise, like giggles in flight,
As fish parade in sheer delight.
A pufferfish, with cheeks so round,
Looks like a balloon that's lost and found.

Hidden treasures sing a tune,
With clams that dance like a cartoon.
Starfish gossip about the tide,
In underwater jest, they confide.

Eels slip by with a wink and grin,
While sand dollars chuckle at the din.
The sea is a stage, fun-filled and bright,
Where every splash adds to the delight.

Tide's Hidden Harmony

The tide rolls in with a belly laugh,
As dolphins play the silly half.
Pigeons strut down the sandy shore,
A feathered troupe with humor galore.

Crabs in tuxedos take center stage,
Performing skits that are all the rage.
Anemones blush in vibrant hues,
Cheering on the shells with their funny views.

The wind hums tunes we can't quite hear,
While seahorses sway, full of cheer.
The sun sets low, casting a beam,
On this oceanic, laughter-filled dream.

Whales echo rhythms of their own,
As hidden jokes are slyly sown.
In the waves, there's always a jest,
The tide knows how to tease and jest.

Secrets Beneath the Waves

Beneath the surface, fish hold chats,
With ancient turtles and their funny hats.
They gossip about who's the fastest swimmer,
While crabs snap claws like a cartoon bumper.

Octopus juggle shells with flair,
While seahorses do their waltz in the air.
Anemones giggle as they sway and spin,
As the clownfish tease, "Come join in the din!"

A dolphin performs tricks with zest,
While stingrays glide like they're on a quest.
Lobsters grumble about dinner plans,
As seaweed dances to the ocean's bands.

So if you dive below and hear a roar,
It's just the laughter from beneath the floor.
Secrets afloat, hidden yet alive,
In the depths of blue, mischief does thrive!

Tides of Time Unraveled

When the tide pulls back, secrets unfold,
Shells giggle softly of stories untold.
Starfish make wishes on warm sandy beds,
While sea cucumbers sip at life's threads.

Time crawls in currents like a snail on a spree,
With clams keeping tabs on the fishery fee.
Hermit crabs move with a curious grace,
Wondering who will take over their space.

Seagulls squawk jokes as they take flight,
While sandpipers prance, what a comical sight!
The tides roll in with a splash and a cheer,
As sea otters frolic, with no hint of fear.

Life ebbs and flows in a comedic dance,
With nature's humor, not left to chance.
So when the tide shifts, just laugh and play,
For the sea knows how to frolic away!

Echoes from the Deep

In the deep blue, where echoes reside,
Mermaids sing songs with a giggle and glide.
Nemo's lost in his favorite game,
As the eels roll their eyes and can't quite explain.

With bubbles that burst like odd little jokes,
Sea lions chuckle and trade their pokes.
The jellyfish sway with grace and delight,
Glowing like lanterns in the soft moonlight.

Coral reefs chortle, bright colors abound,
As fish throw a party, they dance round and round.
The whispers of currents, tales filled with cheer,
Bouncing off barnacles, tickling the ear.

So if you should listen to the sea's gentle hum,
You'll find hidden laughter, oh, so welcome.
For beneath the waves where wonders are steep,
The ocean is filled with its echoes so deep!

The Dance of Distant Shores

On distant shores, the laughter combines,
As seashells hold secrets in playful lines.
Crabs do the moonwalk on shimmering sand,
While seagulls cackle, a feathered band.

Waves whisper jokes as they crash with a splash,
While beach balls bounce like a game gone awash.
The sunset winks with a mischievous grin,
As sun-kissed sandcastles invite us to win.

At sunset's embrace, when the day has died,
Starfish try yoga, relaxing with pride.
As the tide rolls in, stories are spun,
Every ripple a giggle, oh what fun!

So dance with the waves, let your spirit soar,
On distant shores where laughter's never poor.
In the rhythm of foam, joy we'll explore,
As the tide serenades us, forevermore!

Resounding Secrets of the Sea's Heart

Bubbles rise with giggles, so light,
Fish in bow ties dance through the night.
A clam takes a selfie, poses with glee,
While crabs stomp the beat, it's quite a spree!

Whales throw a party, balloons everywhere,
Octopuses juggling, what a wild affair!
The seaweed is swaying, giving a cheer,
As seagulls provide the tunes, oh dear!

The starfish's jokes are always a hit,
Shells laugh so hard, they can't even sit.
The fish flip their tales, oh what a sight,
Underwater shindig, oh, what pure delight!

With shells as the cups, and sand as the cake,
The party will go on till the dawn's first break.
For in this blue world, laughter's the key,
Where secrets abound, oh what fun, you'll see!

Currents Kissing the Kelp Forest

Seahorses waltz, their tails all entwined,
The kelp sways along, unbothered, unlined.
Starfish in tutus, twirl with great pride,
Giggles echo softly, the tide is their guide.

With a tickle of bubbles, the puffer fish grins,
While jellyfish float with their whimsical fins.
Crabs play hopscotch on rocks, what a scene!
The seaweed's a witness, it knows what they mean.

A dolphin's in stripes, oh, what a surprise!
Waves rolling by with mischievous eyes.
Kelp curls its arms, giving hugs all around,
In this underwater dance, joy is profound!

So join in the jigs, let laughter take flight,
In the forest of kelp, everything feels right.
For the ocean holds secrets; it's true, it's a blast,
With currents that kiss—nothing's ever too fast!

The Symphony of Silent Splash

A splash here and there, a drum roll from fish,
The conductor's a crab with a salty old wish.
Clams and mussels, they play the refrain,
While the sea cucumbers join in the fun like a chain.

With a plink and a plonk, the sea otters play,
Their harmonies carried on waves that sway.
The seaweed claps, creating a scene,
As fish wear their hats and play tambourine.

Surfers on bubbles, riding the crest,
While whales in the distance serenely jest.
The rhythm of splash, it's a playful sound,
In the watery theater, joy can be found!

So raise up your fins, let your troubles wash out,
In this crackling concert, there's nothing to doubt.
For here in the depths, life dances and spins,
With laughter that echoes, oh, let the fun begin!

Soliloquies of the Submerged

A turtle prattles on about love for the foam,
While a grouchy old grouper just wants to go home.
Seashells gossip, their stories abound,
Each whisper a treasure, where secrets are found.

Anemones giggle, tickling what's near,
While little fish gossip about their next year.
The sea floor is a stage, with drama so vast,
Where octopuses boast of their adventures past.

A lonely old lobster recites love's great plight,
While corals nod gently, caught up in the night.
The currents weave tales that make everyone laugh,
In this underwater world, enjoy the last half!

So listen closely now, to the splashes and sighs,
For life 'neath the waves is filled with surprise.
Where laughter is heard in every soft swirl,
In soliloquies spoken by the blues and the pearls!

Coves of Enigma and Charm

In cove so snug, the sea turtles grin,
They wear tiny hats, oh where to begin?
With snails in a race on a sandy flat,
They cheer like spectators, imagine that!

A crab in a tux, he dances with flair,
Sipping on seaweed, he's quite the heir!
With fish in tuxedos, they twirl all around,
In watery ballrooms where laughter is found.

A dolphin jumps high, does a flip in the air,
While jellyfish wiggle, with style and care.
The seaweed does salsa, such moves full of zest,
It seems that the sea knows how to impress!

So if you feel blue, just dive in and see,
The whimsical world where fish dance with glee.
Each tile of the ocean hides laughter and cheer,
In coves of enigma, let's toast with a beer!

Harmonies of Movement and Silence

A fishy pianist plays tunes from the deep,
While seahorses waltz, making quite a sweep.
They use tiny shells as musical notes,
With bubbles that pop, like laughter that floats.

The octopus raps with his eight-armed flair,
While starfish just giggle, lying 'round without care.
Anemones sway, like they're in a trance,
As crabs do the twist in a pincer-like dance.

From the depths to the shore, symphonies thrive,
Harmonies bubble where sea creatures jive.
With dolphins that chime and grouper that croon,
It's a melody wild as a beach ball at noon!

So listen quite closely to the waves' gentle hum,
Underwater laughter: it's sheer, frothy fun.
The sea has a rhythm, a funky delight,
Where silence and movement make music each night!

The Secretive Waltz of the Waters

A clam in a cloak, it's quite the disguise,
Peeking at gossip with its tiny eyes.
An eel does the tango in currents so bold,
While sea cucumbers share secrets untold.

With whispers from shells in a clamorous fête,
The sea stars unite, and they dance to their fate.
The fish form a line, doing conga, oh dear!
While sea urchins poke from their corners, in fear.

As surfboards go by, a barnacle sighs,
Wishing for waves, what a shame, it's a lie!
The tide pulls a prank, in a splish and a splash,
While waves roll on through, making bubbles that crash.

So beware of the currents, they'll surely seduce,
With laughter and glee, like a playful excuse.
In secretive waltzes, the waters are clear,
They're hiding their joy, waiting just to appear!

Ephemeral Dances of the Deep

In the depths where the light turns a magical hue,
Dancing plankton gather, oh, what a view!
They twinkle like stars, with a wink and a flash,
In ephemeral dances, they swirl and they thrash.

A narwhal in ballet, with a twirl and a twist,
Too busy to notice that he just got kissed.
With fish in tutus, who knew they could prance?
The water's alive in a whimsical dance!

A squid pens a sonnet with ink and finesse,
He accidentally writes his amorous mess.
While krill do the hustle, in bubbles they burst,
They're partying hard, while the sea snickers first.

So come take a dip, find your rhythm with glee,
Join the creatures who dance in this grand jubilee!
In ephemeral bursts, the ocean will charm,
With laughter and joy, lending all of us calm.

The Submerged Serenade

Beneath the waves, a fish does hum,
Jellyfish jig like they're at a drum,
Seahorses squeal in a wavy dance,
While crabs complain they missed their chance.

Anemones sway in rhythmic glee,
Starfish are arguing over tea,
Clownfish groan at the seaweed mess,
'Can anyone help us? We're in distress!'

Turtles tie bows, looking quite slick,
While octopuses strike with their trick,
The chorus of bubbles, blunders, and grins,
Make the deep sea party begin to spin.

So next time you gaze at the tidal crest,
Remember those sea critters can't rest,
They flip and they flop with a splash and a wink,
Beneath the waves, they're wilder than you think!

Secrets in the Seaweed

In tangled greens, secrets await,
A fish in disguise thinks it's quite great,
'You can't catch me, I'm a slimy ghost!'
Said the sea cucumber, a bragging boast.

Crabs dig deep for a treasure's tease,
While snails gossip about the sea breeze,
What do they find with a laugh and a sneak?
A lost flip-flop, the strangest of peaks!

The seaweed giggles, tickling the snail,
As dolphins leap with a splashy trail,
'Hey, Mr. Lobster, why the scowl?'
'Caught in a seaweed and can't make a howl!'

When waves throw a party, it's nothing but fun,
With sea creatures dancing until they are done,
So who knew the sea had such mischievous plots?
With whispers and laughter, it's all that it's got!

Deep Calls to Deep

In the bathysphere, deep down we go,
Where fish wear hats and green potbelly glow,
Anglerfish giggle with a light on their head,
'Who needs a torch when you've got this thread?'

The echo of bubbles says, 'Dive in with cheer!'
A narwhal chuckles, 'It's cozy down here!'
Corals converse about the latest trend,
'Is this the depth where the charm never ends?'

Puffers puff up just to impress,
While sea slugs slip in sequined dress,
'What's that smell?' asks a dapper mackerel,
'Oh just some seaweed, it's fashion, not feral!'

And if you look closely past the deep blues,
You'll find quirky creatures who choose to amuse,
They're not just there to swim and to creep,
But to live out their dreams where laughter runs deep!

Nautical Whispers

On the deck of a ship, whispers do tread,
A squid tells tales that make everyone dread,
'Why did the fish blush?' it slyly did tease,
'It saw the ocean floor and just couldn't believe!'

Salty seagulls gossip and take to the skies,
While octopus baristas serve drinks with big eyes,
'What do you want, a clam or a shake?'
'Wait, no, I'm on a diet, for goodness' sake!'

Barnacles cling like old friends in a chat,
Saying, 'You're still hanging on? Imagine that!'
And whales sing low, like a song from afar,
While dolphins dance under a glittering star.

So if you venture where the waters are blue,
Don't forget to listen, they want to greet you,
With funny remarks and a nautical cheer,
Life's a big laugh when you dive down here!

The Lure of the Luminous Abyss

In the depths where fishes glow,
A disco party starts to flow,
With jellyfish spinning 'round,
They're the grooviest folks I've found.

A crab walks in with a funky hat,
Says, "Who's got the best dance? Let's chat!"
But they slip and slide on seaweed trails,
Leaving behind a trail of tales.

The octopus shows off its moves,
Ink splatters where nobody grooves,
While sea cucumbers hum a tune,
Swirling 'neath a silver moon.

At the end of night, they bid goodbye,
With sea turtles waving, oh my!
The fish know well how to have fun,
In this bright abyss, always on the run.

Liquid Cadence of the Great Blue

Whales are singing a silly song,
Dolphins giggle, they swim along,
A starfish tries to clap its hands,
While a sea slug executes dance plans.

A pufferfish puffs with such delight,
Saying 'Look at me!' to every fright,
But then a clownfish rolls its eyes,
'You aren't so big, stop with the lies!'

The current's rhythm is quite a tease,
As barbed sea urchins sway with ease,
While seahorses have a jumpy race,
Floating and flailing, oh what a chase!

At the coral disco ball tonight,
Everyone's dancing, it's quite a sight,
With shells and pearls under starlit skies,
The ocean's fun thrives, no goodbyes!

Beneath the Waves, Life Twirls

Beneath the swell, life takes a spin,
A crab does cartwheels, wearing a grin,
With plankton dancers ready to sway,
They shimmy and shake in the bright ballet.

Anemones wave like they're at a show,
While mermaid giggles float to and fro,
"Who lost a bet? What's with that hair?"
As clownfish tease without a care.

A lobster wearing shoes of bright hue,
Struts down the reef; it's a stylish view,
While sea turtles glide, with all their grace,
Dressed to the nines, it's a fancy place!

With bubbles popping and laughter bold,
This underwater world never gets old,
So come for a laugh, dive in the whirl,
Join the parade, where life's a twirl!

Undersea Legends of Yore

Underwater tales, some giggle, some fright,
Of mermaids crafting a seaweed kite,
While fish gossip about the old squid,
Whose ink spills secrets that just can't be hid.

A treasure chest filled with candy and plastic,
Sings sirens' songs, much to its own drastic,
While barnacles argue, who's stuck in a rut,
"Can't we be friends? Let's stop the dispute!"

A whale tells stories of ships gone astray,
With a wink and a snort that makes fish sway,
And all of the crabs remember the night,
When they danced with a mermaid—oh what a sight!

So raise a glass full of seawater cheer,
To legends and laughter, we hold so dear,
For down in the depths, humor's ensured,
In this watery world, we're eternally lured!

Lullabies of the Blue Depths

In deep waters where fish float,
A crab sings tunes in a top hat coat.
The jellyfish dance, so bright and bold,
While seahorses gossip about the cold.

A dolphin juggles shells with glee,
A starfish laughs, 'Hey, look at me!'
The octopus cooks with three pots wide,
While squids perform a flip and glide.

They tell of treasures lost at sea,
But all I found was a heap of brie!
A mermaid claims she's quite the chef,
Her specialty? A fishy quiche, no less!

So if you hear a wave that giggles,
It's just the sea making silly wiggles.
Underwater tales that tickle the ear,
In depths of laughter, let's disappear!

The Veins of Aqua Earth

Coral reefs, like traffic lanes,
Fish honk horns with silly refrains.
Turtles race in a sassy way,
While crabs strut like they own the bay.

Seaweed sways, a curtain call,
"Who ordered this!" a fish does bawl.
The angler fish with lights so bright,
Says, "I'm just here for the nightlife!"

A puffin burps a bubble loud,
As clownfish put on quite the crowd.
A whale with rhythm starts to groove,
While sea stars make a dance move.

Beneath the waves, it's quirky fun,
Each wave a joke, each splash a pun.
A fizzle, a sizzle, laughter's theme,
In watery realms where fishy dreams!

Mysteries Veiled in Aquamarine

What's that lurking in the gloom?
A pufferfish in a paper bloom!
The lobsters argue, "Who took my hat?"
A clam just shrugs, "Well, isn't that cr**?"

Schools of fish, they in a line,
Stumbling around, they can't define.
"Where'd we go? What's this place?"
The shrimp just giggles, "It's a funny face!"

A hidden world with quirky sights,
Where sea cucumbers have disco nights.
Anemones wave like they're on parade,
Counting all the friends they've made.

Whispers from the sea foam spray,
"Join our party and dance all day!"
Underwater secrets, ticklish delight,
In the splash of waves, the mood feels right.

Cascading Secrets of the Salty Sea

Waves tumble down with little giggles,
While fish tell tales, and sea turtles wiggle.
A splash, a dash, what tricks they pull,
A fisherman's net? Just a shiny jewel!

Barnacles chime with a rusty tune,
"Get your shells, let's start a commune!"
A whale joins in with a belly laugh,
Drawing hearts in water with a playful craft.

Zany sea urchins, quirky brigade,
"Let's have a contest for the best charade!"
The kraken brings snacks—what a treat,
While pet fish wear hats, oh so neat!

In frothy waves, the laughter swirls,
Each bubble bursts with playful pearls.
A party down where the sun can't see,
The salty sea, where wild winds spree!

Chasms of Solitude

In the depths, there's a clam with flair,
Dancing solo, without a care.
A fish trips over its own two fins,
While laughing at the octopus's spins.

A crab dreams of being more than shells,
Takes tap dance lessons, and jigs so well.
But seaweed keeps getting in the way,
So he waltzes off—'I'm done for today!'

The turtles throw a disco ball,
While gulls crash parties and take a fall.
Seagulls squawking about their prime time,
As the plankton applaud every rhyme.

So here's to the goofs down below,
Where merriment and chaos grow.
If you seek a laugh in the deep blue,
Just swim with the fish, they're funny too!

The Soul of the Sea

There's a whale who tells dad jokes galore,
Every splash has the fish begging for more.
He's got a punchline that's hard to believe,
As he sings of a shark that doesn't deceive.

A starfish gives a wave, struck by the thought,
'Why is it hard for me to get caught?'
It's because he's got five handy hands,
Practicing yoga with seaweed strands.

Coral reefs throw a party at night,
With lanterns aglow, it's quite the sight.
Anemones dance in a rhythmic flair,
While a dolphin attempts a pirouette rare.

So gather 'round for the oceanic cheer,
With fishy friends who are always near.
Life down here is a laugh-filled spree,
Join the fun—it's silly as can be!

Mysteries in the Brine

A sea cucumber hides his face with fear,
Claims he's the best at playing the sphere.
Yet every time he throws it about,
He just ends up stuck—oh, what a clout!

A pirate fish, he thinks he's so sly,
Hiding treasures beneath the vast sky.
But his booty? Just rocks all around,
As he swims with great pride—what a clown!

A mussel writes poems beneath the waves,
But they're all cult classics, hardly raves.
He recites them to shrimps who just roll,
While a crab yells mockingly, 'Aren't we all full?'

So swim through the depths, let laughter unite,
In the mysteries where sea critters ignite.
Their shenanigans keep us chasing the tide,
For joy in the brine, there's nothing to hide!

Melodies in the Salt

The sea sings a tune, or so they say,
But it's really just seahorses, lost in ballet.
They swish and sway in a fashion bizarre,
While crabs take videos, 'Look at them star!'

A jellyfish jiggles with all of its might,
Flashing its colors—what a dance at night!
A shrimp joins in, clacking his claws,
While a fish laughs out loud, 'And here are my flaws!'

An octopus plays maracas with glee,
Whispers to sand dollars, 'Just dance with me!'
But sand dollars rolled away in fright,
Leaving the octopus alone in the night.

So join in the rhythm, feel the delight,
In the salty sea where laughter takes flight.
For hidden in the waves, there's a jolly spree,
As nature's own band plays a tune just for thee!

Murmurs in the Marine Night

The fish all gather round, quite sly,
Telling tales of ships that fly.
They wiggle and giggle in their finned attire,
While crabs conduct a crustacean choir.

Stars above, they twinkle bright,
While dolphins dance with sheer delight.
A seaweed wig is all the rage,
As octopuses take the stage.

A whale rolls by, a gentle grunt,
Spooking shrimp with just a stunt.
A sea anemone starts a joke,
But seashells laugh until they choke.

Bubbles rise with every tease,
As turtles join in, aiming to please.
In the deep, the chatter buzzes,
With squid's wild ink making all the fuzzes.

Beneath the Surface

Coral reefs, they paint a scene,
But fish can't stop their little bean.
They gather for a college prank,
And send a turtle to the tank.

A lobster wears a fuzzy hat,
Trying to look like a cool cat.
Jellyfish float, but don't get too close,
One sting, and you'll just cry, "Oh, gross!"

A clam snores loudly, what a sound,
While sea cucumbers roll on the ground.
Octopus juggling with flair and wit,
Might make you laugh until you quit.

The sunken treasure's just a prop,
Where seahorses swarm, performing the hop.
Underwater giggles, what a delight,
Beneath the waves, all's dynamic and bright.

Silence Speaks

In waters deep, silence reigns,
But not for long, here comes the chains.
Sea turtles with gossip, who won the race,
While conch shells think they rule the place.

Anemones start a garden trend,
Sharing secrets they cannot bend.
Clownfish chuckle, hiding their glee,
As they play peekaboo, oh so free.

Shrimps host parties, just for laughs,
They recruit all the best underwater staff.
A dance battle ignites with flair,
But an octopus outshines in mid-air.

Whales are the judges, very stern,
Determining who'll win, and twist and turn.
But under the quiet, laughter's a song,
In the silence of the sea, where we all belong.

The Rhythm of Salty Breath

The tide rolls in with whispers sweet,
Where barnacles cling to each fish's feet.
A sea bass struts, thinks it's a star,
While plankton dance in a wild bazaar.

Sea otters juggle with shells and grace,
Filling the deep with a laugh-filled space.
The rhythm of waves and flippers collide,
A joyful mashup, a slippery ride.

A hermit crab, in borrowed shoes,
Shows off his stuff, has nothing to lose.
Starfish cheer, they can't sit still,
Transforming the floor into a thrill.

From the kelp, the laughter echoes loud,
As fish swim free, so proud, so proud!
With bubbles bursting at every glance,
The salty breath inspires the dance.

In the Shadow of Coral Castles

Beneath coral towers that twist and twine,
The sea critters gather, all feeling fine.
A pufferfish struts, wearing a crown,
While sea urchins poke, making the rounds.

Clownfish tell jokes, making others beam,
Their antics can make you laugh 'til you scream.
Shrimps play bumper, in a game so sleek,
While algae watches, almost too chic.

The coral spaghetti becomes a buffet,
As seahorses waltz, 'neath the waves they sway.
In shadows, they sway, without a care,
With humor unfolding in that salty air.

A dolphin skims by, cracking a grin,
Singing a ditty on a playful whim.
In the depths where the laughter flows,
In this underwater realm, anything goes!

Cradle of the Abyss

In the deep where mermaids play,
They dance and sip on salty spray.
With fishy friends, they spin and twirl,
Swapping tails in a swirly whirl.

An octopus juggles pearls like a clown,
A sea turtle wears a fancy crown.
With seaweed wigs and laughter loud,
The ocean's depths can be quite proud.

Nautical pranks like hide-and-seek,
With playful waves that gently speak.
They tickle sharks and tease the rays,
In the darkest depths where laughter sways.

So let's splash into this watery jest,
Where bubbles burst and fish are best.
The undersea antics bring us glee,
In the cradle of the deep sea spree.

The Untold Symphony of Water

Bubbles pop in a jazzy tune,
A dolphin croons beneath the moon.
Octaves rise like swirling foam,
In this liquid world we call home.

Crabs tap dance on the sandy shore,
While clams hum soft tunes, wanting more.
The seaweed sways with all its might,
In this underwater Friday night.

A whale's deep voice starts the show,
While fish swim fast in a synchrony flow.
Jellyfish float like tranquil dreams,
In a sea of laughter, bursting seams.

So grab a shell, let's join the band,
In this ocean symphony, so grand.
Where rhythm and splash create delight,
In the depths where giggles take flight.

Whispers of the Abyss

The fish gossip in colorful haste,
About a crab who can't find the taste.
He tried sushi, but oh what a mess,
A crab who can't cook? What a distress!

Anemones giggle, tickling the sea,
As a silly clownfish swims with glee.
A starfish jokes, "I can't even flex!"
With five arms, you'd think he's complex!

Eels whisper secrets, lurking around,
While jellyfish float without a sound.
They play hide and seek but no one can see,
The laughter bubbles in the deep spree.

So next time you dip your toes in blue,
Remember the whispers, secrets, and hue.
In the vibrant depths where humor thrums,
Life beneath the waves is full of fun.

Currents of Forgotten Dreams

The tide brings stories from long ago,
Of pirates who danced with an errant go.
With treasure maps marked with silly signs,
And quests for gold in tangled lines.

A sea horse dreams of being a knight,
But struggles with armor that's just too tight.
With a bubble sword, he takes a stance,
But falls back with a clumsy prance.

Mermaids sing of lost socks and shoes,
With sock puppets on a raucous cruise.
In the swirling currents, laughter grows,
As dreams ride the waves where no one knows.

So let's dive deep with joy and cheer,
Where currents carry our laughter near.
In whimsical waters where secrets gleam,
Swim on through this world of shared dreams.

Deep Blue Reveries

Bubbles rise with laughter, they tickle the toes,
Fish in bow ties swim, pretending they know.
Seahorses dance slowly, with a clumsy flair,
And crabs throw a party, with snacks to spare.

Octopuses juggle, with their wiggly arms,
While turtles debate, with goofy charms.
A dolphin takes selfies, with a wink and a smile,
As a shrimp does a shimmy, in trendy style.

Jellyfish are the drummers, pulsating away,
While starfish cheer loudly, "Hip hip, hooray!"
The coral sings out tunes, a whimsical band,
As the mariners shuffle, across the soft sand.

Underwater dreams bloom, in colors so bright,
With laughter and giggles, from morning 'til night.
In this amusing realm, where mischief runs free,
The hidden joys of the deep, are a sight to see.

Notes from the Ocean's Lowlands

In the shallows, there's chatter, from clams and their clique,
They gossip of whales, who wiggle and sneak.
A flounder's a painter, with a funny old brush,
While sea cucumbers giggle, in a stylish hush.

Starfish wear sunglasses, looking oh-so-fly,
Pools of seaweed dance, under the sunlit sky.
A puffer fish balloons, for a laugh or a scare,
As a shrimp holds a mic, to declare, "Who's there?"

The settlements rustle, with tales that they weave,
Of pirate ghosts buried, who sneeze and then leave.
A charming old grouper tells stories of yore,
While lobsters do limber, on a seabed floor.

In this vibrant abyss, where nothings amiss,
The tides tickle secrets, delights we can't dismiss.
With whimsy abounding, in currents and waves,
There's joy in the laughter of maritime braves.

The Pulse of the Engulfing Deep

Whales wear their tuxedos, for a gala tonight,
Crabs conduct orchestras, with pinchers held tight.
Anglerfish flash smiles, with their glowing dear,
As sea turtles take turns, for the coolest cheer.

Eels tell some tall tales, with a dramatic flair,
While oysters spill secrets, like bubbles in air.
A clownfish is chuckling, as actors at sea,
Each wave breaks with laughter, a whimsical spree.

Coral reefs gossip about the latest trends,
With shells making bets, on which way the tide bends.
Starfish throw confetti, from their sandy retreats,
As seahorses float by in their fanciest feats.

The deep holds its mirth, in a splashy ballet,
With mischief and melodies, swirling all day.
Beneath the blue surface, a party ignites,
Where laughter and joy are the ultimate sights!

Waves of Hidden Narratives

On the crest of a wave, a sea otter's glee,
Juggling bright shells, oh, what a sight to see!
The krill have a bar; they serve tiny drinks,
While lobsters do stand-up, with hilarious winks.

Dolphins engage in a splashy debate,
On who swims the fastest, is it fate or just weight?
A school of fish whispers of gossip so grand,
With turtlenecks on turtles, making waves in the sand.

Anemones wave, tossing praises around,
For the clowns in the ocean, where laughter is found.
A conch holds a concert, with music so sweet,
While crabs stomp a rhythm, tapping their feet.

With stories entwined, in the ebb and the flow,
The charm of the deep brings a glimmering glow.
For every wave hides a giggle or two,
In the vast underwater, where antics renew.

Shadows Beneath the Foam

The fish swim by in a grand parade,
Wearing sunglasses, they look quite made.
An octopus juggles with great delight,
While the crab takes selfies, it's quite the sight.

But wait! There's something hiding below,
A treasure chest with a giant glow.
It's filled with socks, mismatched, of course,
The mermaids giggle, "What's this farce?"

A sea turtle glides with flair so great,
Challenging fish for the fastest plate.
Everyone laughs as the seaweed sways,
In this underwater circus that plays.

So next time you dip in the waves that sway,
Remember the antics of sea life at play.
They might be swimming in serious guise,
But beneath the foam, it's all a surprise!

Breath of the Salted Air

I walked down where the gulls take flight,
They scream at my fries, oh what a sight!
The breeze comes in, with a salty jest,
I offer them crumbs; they're on a quest.

A seaside clam invites me to dine,
Says, "Join me for chowder; it's simply divine!"
But it turns out, it's just full of sand,
I'd rather have chips from the local stand.

The seaweed dances, giving quite the show,
A spectacular twist, who knew it could flow?
The dolphins leap like they're on a spree,
Waving at surfers, "Come ride with me!"

So next time you breathe in that ocean air,
Remember the humor that's floating out there.
From seagulls to clams, they all have a flair,
In a world of salt, laughter's the affair!

The Ocean's Secret Cadence

Deep down where the treasure map is drawn,
A whale tells jokes from dusk until dawn.
"Why did the shark cross the reef?" he grins,
"To show the pufferfish all his fins!"

In caverns, the lobsters hold a grande ball,
They twirl like dancers, having a ball.
A shrimp spins round, it's quite the finesse,
While the swordfish judges, wearing a dress.

The secrets lie in the bubbles they make,
Echoing chuckles with every break.
Turtles do stand-up, cracking the shell,
"Oh, it's hard to tell if I'm coming or well!"

So listen close to the giggles below,
The rhythm of water, its antics will flow.
In depths where you'd think it's all serious fare,
The ocean's humor dances everywhere!

Guardians of the Deep

In the depths where the critters reside,
The fish form a council, taking each side.
They argue, they bubble, they squirt, and they cheer,
"Who guards the deep? Let's make it clear!"

The jellyfish claim they're the wisest of all,
They float with such grace, they never fall.
"Look at us glow!" they boast with great pride,
"Who needs armor when you've got such a tide?"

"The clownfish wins," the octopus said,
Surfacing boldly, with pearls in his head.
"After all, who else can do such a dance,
In a world of bubbles, we'll take our stance!"

From the depths comes a bubble, a burst full of cheer,
"Let's all be friends, there's nothing to fear!"
So next time you surf on a bright sunny day,
Just know the guardians are laughing away!

Sirens of the Silent Deep

In waters bright where laughter thrums,
Mermaids giggle, strumming drums.
They steal your fries, swim off too quick,
Leaving you puzzled, feeling slick.

A fish in shades of neon bright,
Dances like it's Friday night.
A crab in shades of polka dot,
Tries to join, but trips a lot.

Shells sport tattoos no one can see,
Where seaweed sways as if to agree.
Octopuses juggle with flair and wink,
Making waves, who needs to think?

But beware the bubble-blowing squid,
That pops and says, "You've been hid!"
They whisper tales, oh-so-intricate,
While we just laugh and speculate.

Driftwood Stories on the Shore

A log with tales of sunken ships,
Claims it's sailed on daring trips.
But seagulls shout in loud dispute,
"You just floated, you old brute!"

An old shoe tells a tale of woe,
Of being tossed, then left to glow.
A barnacle says, "I'll eat your lace!"
As tides come in, and boats embrace.

Sandcastles rise with royal flair,
While crabs declare, "We own this square!"
A seashell scoffs, "It's mine to keep!"
As kids just giggle, lost in sleep.

Each driftwood piece, a riddle made,
With every wave, new games are played.
So join the fun, let worries soar,
In stories past and tales of yore.

Dance of Marine Mysteries

The jellyfish waltz with grace and flair,
While fish in tuxedos float through air.
Turtles slow-dance in gentle spins,
As dolphins moonwalk with cheeky grins.

A shark in shades thinks it's too cool,
Swims through seas like a backyard pool.
Although he's tough, he's really shy,
"I just want sushi!", is his cry.

Starfish breakdance on the ocean floor,
As plankton twirl and ask for more.
The currents twine like ribbons tight,
While crabs do the cha-cha in delight.

Then a sea lion joins the spree,
Singing songs of salty glee.
The tide rolls in, applauding all,
In waves of joy, we heed the call!

Enigmas of the Endless Blue

In depths where laughter meets the gloom,
A fish sets up an underwater room.
With bubbles as balloons, it's quite a scene,
Where silence sways in shades of green.

A clam plays tricks, the best of all,
It opens wide, then slams with gall.
A sea urchin dons a jester's cap,
Making puns while filling in the gap.

Bubbles float like dreams so bright,
A sea cucumber dreams of flight.
But with each wave that rolls and dips,
It shrugs and decides to take more trips.

The ocean whispers, "Join this play,
Find wonders tucked in every spray."
So dive right in, don't miss the fun,
For hidden laughs, we're not yet done!

Heartbeats of the Vast Expanse

The wave's a dancer, with a splashy flair,
It jives along, with frothy hair.
Each ripple giggles, in the sun's good light,
While crabs play tag, oh, what a sight!

Seagulls squawk with laughter in the breeze,
As fish swim by, doing backflips with ease.
A clam tells secrets, with a sulky frown,
While seaweed twirls like a wild, green gown.

The boat rides rocky, but has quite the bounce,
All aboard are screaming, "Just let me pounce!"
Spray in the air, we're all feeling bold,
As the sun dips low, casting soft gold.

Yet when the tide retreats, we'll have some fun,
Finding odd shells, and the sand dollar's run.
So let's keep dancing, not miss the zest,
In vast blue laughter, life's at its best!

Shadows in the Tide Pools

Tide pools bubble with a splishy sound,
Where tiny critters dance all around.
Starfish wear smiles, both goofy and wide,
While anemones wave like they're trying to hide.

The hermit crabs march in a tiny parade,
Thinking the beach is a grand charade.
Each shell tells tales of what used to roam,
Now sitting lonely in their watery home.

A jellyfish floats with a jelly-filled grace,
As little fish dart in a wild, cramped space.
The sun paints shadows, all funny-shaped,
As crabs start tap-dancing, no plans escaped.

So let's gather 'round and point with glee,
At this silly ocean, so full of spree.
With creatures that giggle in their own ways,
It's hard to tell if it's night or those rays!

Beneath the Cresting Foam

Beneath the waves, it's a bubbly affair,
Where fish wear hats that they craft with care.
Octopuses juggle with a flair so fine,
While shrimp host parties — don't dare decline!

The conch shells gossip about currents and tides,
Every secret, a tale that joyfully glides.
Sea cucumbers fashion the latest trends,
In this underwater world, where fun never ends.

A dolphin chases fairytales in bliss,
With a playful flip, you wouldn't want to miss.
As coral reefs giggle in technicolor hues,
Life's a wacky party — nothing to lose!

So dive down deep, let the laughter roll,
In the heart of the waves, find your joyful soul.
With each splash a chuckle, oh, what a thrill,
The deep blue laughter, it gives us a chill!

The Call of Distant Horizons

Where the sky meets the sea, in a drifty dance,
The breeze feels playful, it's your lucky chance!
Sailing toward laughter, with wind in our hair,
Every wave's a wink, a cheeky affair.

The horizon teases with a bright shining light,
Promising giggles, from morning till night.
And every leaf boat, in the marsh nearby,
Is dreaming of journeys beneath a blue sky.

With whales that sing tunes only dolphins know,
Their melodies echo, creating a show.
You'll find silly mermaids, all clad in shells,
As they crack up the coast with their comical spells.

So follow that laughter out to the brink,
Where the salty air makes you stop and think.
This curious world pulls you far from your care,
With each wave's whisper, it's time to prepare!

Submerged Echoes of Eternity

Bubbles rise with a giggling sound,
Fish are ticklish, who knew they abound?
Coral reefs dance to a jellyfish song,
When seaweed sways, you can't go wrong!

A crab with a hat struts down the lane,
Shimmies and shakes, what a funny gain!
Octopus juggling, he steals the show,
Claps from the clams; it's quite the flow!

Whales telling jokes, their laughs are vast,
Splashing the sharks, oh my, what a contrast!
Seahorses gossip while sipping some tea,
In this underwater realm, laughter is free!

Eels twist and shout with a jolly good cheer,
Manta rays spin, making quite clear,
In their blue kingdom, it's all quite a fuss,
Life under waves, so amusing for us!

Murmurs in the Tide

Waves are whispering tales of delight,
Crabs in a conga, what a silly sight!
Starfish counting their legs on a breeze,
Sea turtles giggling at jokes with ease!

A dolphin detours to join in the fun,
Doing backflips, oh how they run!
Lobsters in bow ties, quite dapper and spry,
Dancing to rhythms under the sky!

With a flip and a flounder, the fish take flight,
Pirates' old treasure chests giggle with fright!
Fish using bubbles to burst out a tune,
Underwater comedy, a whimsical boon!

Eddy the eel with a pun in his grin,
Promises laughter each time he swims in,
Jellyfish flicker, they light up the night,
Waves of hilarity, a true ocean delight!

Veils of Water and Wonder

In the depths, where laughter sneaks,
Anglerfish prank on the shy critters' peaks,
Squid in a tux, ready for a dance,
Tickling the seabed, they prance and prance!

Grouchy old crabs, they grumble and pout,
Caught in a bubble, oh what a clout!
Seahorses dressed up in outfits so bright,
Compete for the crown in their vibrant light!

Clams reciting poems, clapping their shells,
Performing for fish, with giggles and yells,
Anemones wave like they're hosting a show,
Tides of humor where silliness flows!

Sharks with a secret, they're really quite shy,
Only want hugs, and maybe a fry,
As currents giggle and silt swirls around,
Joy in the depths is resoundingly found!

Fluid Melodies of the Underworld

An orchestra of bubbles in the swell,
Fiddler crabs make quite the noise, oh swell!
Flying fish take off, oh what a flight,
In schools of laughter, they swoop and bite!

Blowfish puff up to join in the scene,
Making bold faces, quite a marine routine.
Eels play the strings while the plankton sing,
A festival of fun in this underwater fling!

Gurgles and giggles echo through the foam,
Every fish feels right at home!
Tangled in seaweed, they laugh and roll,
Making waves of joy that tickle the soul!

With each playful lure and twist of the caress,
The deep blue hides a world full of jest,
From bubbles to chuckles, the currents chase,
Underneath all the surface, a smile finds its place!